Dear God

By

T. J. Wilson

This Book is Dedicated to:
GOD WHO WAS ALWAYS THERE NO MATTER WHAT I DID
TO MY PARENTS WHO WERE CHRISTIANS
MY DAUGHTHER JESSICA WHO GOT ME STARTED IN CHURCH
TO MY SON RICHARD WHO HAS FOUND THE LORD
TO MY SISTER EMMA WHO ALWAYS TALKED ABOUT CHURCH
TO MY GRANDDAUGHTER KYRIA WHOM I LOVE

COVER DESIGN LULU
BACK DESIGN LULU

Acknowledgements
To those in my life that keep me on the straight and
narrow path.

If Quotations are from the New American Standard Bible (1995 Updated Edition):
"Scripture taken from the *NEW AMERICAN STANDARD BIBLE®*,
© Copyright 1960, 1962, 1963, 1968, 1971, 1972, 1973, 1975, 1977, 1995 by The Lockm
Foundation
Used by permission." (www.Lockman.org)

Published by T.J. Wilson
Cincinnati, Oh
978-0-6151-7044-2

DEAR GOD,

If anyone is in Christ, [he is] a new
creature; the old things passed away; behold,
new things have come.
2 Corinthians 5:17 (Read all of
2 Corinthians 5)
New American Standard Bible

DEAR GOD,

_____
_____
_____
_____
_____
_____
_____
_____
_____
_____
_____
_____
_____
_____

Even a fool, when he keeps silent, is
considered wise; When he closes his lips, he
is [considered] prudent.
Proverbs 17:28 (Read all of Proverbs 17)
New American Standard Bible

DEAR GOD,

_____
_____
_____
_____
_____
_____
_____
_____
_____
_____
_____
_____
_____
_____

Who is a God like You, who pardons iniquity
And passes over the rebellious act of the
remnant of His possession? He does not retain
His anger forever, Because He delights in
unchanging love.
Micah 7:18 (Read all of Micah 7)
New American Standard Bible

This Book Belongs To:

To those who do not know how to pray, but who want to speak to GOD

Write your prayers down and he will read them. This copy in NSAV version

DEAR GOD,

_____
_____
_____
_____
_____
_____
_____
_____
_____
_____
_____
_____
_____
_____
_____
_____
_____
_____

For the wages of sin is death, but the free
gift of God is eternal life in Christ Jesus
our Lord.
Romans 6:23 (Read all of Romans 6)
New American Standard Bible

DEAR GOD,

_____

_____

_____

_____

_____

_____

_____

_____

_____

_____

_____

_____

_____

_____

For in it [the] righteousness of God is
revealed from faith to faith; as it is
written, "BUT THE RIGHTEOUS [man] SHALL LIVE
BY FAITH."
Romans 1:17 (Read all of Romans 1)
New American Standard Bible

DEAR GOD,

_____
_____
_____
_____
_____
_____
_____
_____
_____
_____
_____
_____
_____
_____

For since the creation of the world His
invisible attributes, His eternal power and
divine nature, have been clearly seen, being
understood through what has been made, so
that they are without excuse.
Romans 1:20 (Read all of Romans 1)
New American Standard Bible

DEAR GOD,

_____
_____
_____
_____
_____
_____
_____
_____
_____
_____
_____
_____

For a day in Your courts is better than a thousand [outside.] I would rather stand at the threshold of the house of my God Than dwell in the tents of wickedness.
Psalm 84:10 (Read all of
Psalm 84)
New American Standard Bible

DEAR GOD,

_____
_____
_____
_____
_____
_____
_____
_____
_____
_____
_____
_____
_____
_____

Or do you not know that the unrighteous will not inherit the kingdom of God? Do not be deceived; neither fornicators, nor idolaters, nor adulterers, nor effeminate, nor homosexuals,
1 Corinthians 6:9 (Read all of
1 Corinthians 6)
New American Standard Bible

DEAR GOD,

The one who guards his mouth preserves his
life; The one who opens wide his lips comes
to ruin.
Proverbs 13:3 (Read all of Proverbs 13)
New American Standard Bible

DEAR GOD,

_____
_____
_____
_____
_____
_____
_____
_____
_____
_____
_____
_____
_____
_____
_____
_____
_____
_____
_____
_____
_____

What is desirable in a man is his kindness.
Proverbs 19:22a (Read all of Proverbs 19)
New American Standard Bible

DEAR GOD,

_____

_____

_____

_____

_____

_____

_____

_____

_____

_____

_____

_____

_____

_____

_____

"Blessed are the peacemakers, for they shall
be called sons of God."
Matthew 5:9 (Read all of Matthew 5)
New American Standard Bible

DEAR GOD,

_____
_____
_____
_____
_____
_____
_____
_____
_____
_____
_____
_____
_____
_____
_____
_____
_____
_____

Daniel prayed, "Let the name of God be blessed forever and ever, For wisdom and power belong to Him.
Daniel 2:20 (Read all of Daniel 2)
New American Standard Bible

DEAR GOD,

_____
_____
_____
_____
_____
_____
_____
_____
_____
_____
_____
_____
_____
_____
_____

For we all stumble in many [ways.] If anyone
does not stumble in what he says, he is a
perfect man, able to bridle the whole body as
well.
James 3:2 (Read all of James 3)
New American Standard Bible

DEAR GOD,

_____
_____
_____
_____
_____
_____
_____
_____
_____
_____
_____
_____
_____
_____

Instead of your shame [you will have a]
double [portion,] And [instead of]
humiliation they will shout for joy over
their portion. Therefore they will possess a
double [portion] in their land, Everlasting
joy will be theirs.
Isaiah 61:7 (Read all of Isaiah 61)
New American Standard Bible

DEAR GOD,

_____

_____

_____

_____

_____

_____

_____

_____

_____

_____

_____

The Spirit of the Lord GOD
is upon me, Because the LORD has anointed me
To bring good news to the afflicted; He has
sent me to bind up the brokenhearted, To
proclaim liberty to captives And freedom to
prisoners;
Isaiah 61:1 (Read all of Isaiah 61)
New American Standard Bible

DEAR GOD,

_____
_____
_____
_____
_____
_____
_____
_____
_____
_____
_____
_____
_____
_____
_____
_____
_____
_____
_____
_____

"For what does it profit a man to gain the
whole world, and forfeit his soul?"
Mark 8:36 (Read all of Mark 8)
New American Standard Bible

DEAR GOD,

_____
_____
_____
_____
_____
_____
_____
_____
_____
_____
_____
_____
_____

Indeed, [while following] the way of Your judgments, O LORD, We have waited for You eagerly; Your name, even Your memory, is the desire of [our] souls.
Isaiah 26:8 (Read all of Isaiah 26)
New American Standard Bible

DEAR GOD,

_____

_____

_____

_____

_____

_____

_____

_____

_____

_____

_____

_____

_____

_____

_____

_____

_____

A perverse man spreads strife, And a
slanderer separates intimate friends.
Proverbs 16:28 (Read all of Proverbs 16)
New American Standard Bible

DEAR GOD,

_____
_____
_____
_____
_____
_____
_____
_____
_____
_____
_____
_____
_____
_____
_____
_____

Better is a poor man who walks in his
integrity Than he who is perverse in speech
and is a fool.
Proverbs 19:1 (Read all of Proverbs 19)
New American Standard Bible

DEAR GOD,

_____
_____
_____
_____
_____
_____
_____
_____
_____
_____
_____
_____
_____
_____
_____
_____
_____

So, as those who have been chosen of God,
holy and beloved, put on a heart of
compassion, kindness, humility, gentleness
and patience;
Colossians 3:12 (Read all of Colossians 3)
New American Standard Bible

DEAR GOD,

_____

_____

_____

_____

_____

_____

_____

_____

_____

_____

_____

For this, "YOU SHALL NOT
COMMIT ADULTERY, YOU SHALL NOT MURDER, YOU
SHALL NOT STEAL, YOU SHALL NOT COVET," and if
there is any other commandment, it is summed
up in this saying, "YOU SHALL LOVE YOUR
NEIGHBOR AS YOURSELF."
Romans 13:9 (Read all of Romans 13)
New American Standard Bible

DEAR GOD,

_____
_____
_____
_____
_____
_____
_____
_____
_____
_____
_____
_____
_____
_____
_____
_____

Every person is to be in subjection to the
governing authorities. For there is no
authority except from God, and those which
exist are established by God..
Romans 13:1 (Read all of Romans 13)
New American Standard Bible

DEAR GOD,

Blessed is a man who perseveres under trial;
for once he has been approved, he will
receive the crown of life which [the Lord]
has promised to those who love Him.
James 1:12 (Read all of James 1)
New American Standard Bible

DEAR GOD,

_____
_____
_____
_____
_____
_____
_____
_____
_____
_____
_____
_____
_____
_____
_____
_____
_____

"Give
to everyone who asks of you, and whoever
takes away what is yours, do not demand it
back."
Luke 6:30 (Read all of Luke 6)
New American Standard Bible

DEAR GOD,

_____
_____
_____
_____
_____
_____
_____
_____
_____
_____
_____
_____
_____
_____
_____
_____
_____

"Comfort, O comfort My people," says your
God.
Isaiah 40:1 (Read all of Isaiah 40)
New American Standard Bible

DEAR GOD,

_____
_____
_____
_____
_____
_____
_____
_____
_____
_____
_____
_____
_____
_____
_____
_____
_____
_____
_____

The world is passing away, and [also] its
lusts; but the one who does the will of God
lives forever.
1 John 2:17 (Read all of 1 John 2)
New American Standard Bible

DEAR GOD,

_____

_____

_____

_____

_____

_____

_____

_____

_____

_____

_____

_____

_____

_____

_____

Many
are the sorrows of the wicked, But he who
trusts in the LORD, lovingkindness shall
surround him.
Psalm 32:10 (Read all of Psalm 32)
New American Standard Bible

DEAR GOD,

_____
_____
_____
_____
_____
_____
_____
_____
_____
_____
_____
_____
_____
_____
_____
_____
_____
_____

Now, little children, abide in Him, so that
when He appears, we may have confidence and
not shrink away from Him in shame at His
coming.
1 John 2:28 (Read all of 1 John 2)
New American Standard Bible

DEAR GOD,

_____

_____

_____

_____

_____

_____

_____

_____

_____

_____

_____

_____

_____

_____

Now may the God of hope fill you with all joy
and peace in believing, so that you will
abound in hope by the power of the Holy
Spirit.
Romans 15:13 (Read all of Romans 15)
New American Standard Bible

DEAR GOD,

_____

_____

_____

_____

_____

_____

_____

_____

_____

_____

_____

_____

_____

_____

_____

_____

_____

_____

_____

This is the message we have
heard from Him and announce to you, that God
is Light, and in Him there is no darkness at
all.
1 John 1:5 (Read all of 1 John 1)
New American Standard Bible

DEAR GOD,

_____
_____
_____
_____
_____
_____
_____
_____
_____
_____
_____
_____
_____
_____
_____

The things you have learned and received and
heard and seen in me, practice these things,
and the God of peace will be with you.
Philippians 4:9 (Read all of Philippians 4)
New American Standard Bible

DEAR GOD,

_____
_____
_____
_____
_____
_____
_____
_____
_____
_____
_____
_____
_____
_____
_____
_____
_____
_____
_____
_____
_____

Whatever you do, do your work heartily, as
for the Lord rather than for men,.
Colossians 3:23 (Read all of Colossians 3)
New American Standard Bible

DEAR GOD,

The Law came in so that the transgression
would increase; but where sin increased,
grace abounded all the more,
Romans 5:20 (Read all of Romans 5)
New American Standard Bible

DEAR GOD,

Your word I have treasured in
my heart, That I may not sin against You.
Psalm 119:11 (Read all of Psalm 119)
New American Standard Bible

DEAR GOD,

_____
_____
_____
_____
_____
_____
_____
_____
_____
_____
_____
_____
_____
_____

'Behold, I stand at the door and knock; if
anyone hears My voice and opens the door, I
will come in to him and will dine with him,
and he with Me.
Revelation 3:20 (Read all of Revelation 3)
New American Standard Bible

DEAR GOD,

_____
_____
_____
_____
_____
_____
_____
_____
_____
_____
_____
_____
_____
_____
_____
_____
_____
_____
_____
_____

When I am afraid, I will put my trust in You.
Psalm 56:3 (Read all of Psalm 56)
New American Standard Bible

DEAR GOD,

_____

_____

_____

_____

_____

_____

_____

_____

_____

_____

And
My people who are called by My name humble
themselves and pray and seek My face and turn
from their wicked ways, then I will hear from
heaven, will forgive their sin and will heal
their land.
2 Chronicles 7:14 (Read all of
2 Chronicles 7)
New American Standard Bible

DEAR GOD,

_____
_____
_____
_____
_____
_____
_____
_____
_____
_____
_____
_____
_____
_____
_____
_____
_____
_____
_____

Jesus said to her, "Did I not say to you that
if you believe, you will see the glory of
God?"
John 11:40 (Read all of John 11)
New American Standard Bible

DEAR GOD,

_____
_____
_____
_____
_____
_____
_____
_____
_____
_____
_____
_____

Then the Lord said,
"Because this people draw near with their
words And honor Me with their lip service,
But they remove their hearts far from Me, And
their reverence for Me consists of tradition
learned [by rote,]
Isaiah 29:13 (Read all of Isaiah 29)
New American Standard Bible

DEAR GOD,

_____
_____
_____
_____
_____
_____
_____
_____
_____
_____
_____
_____
_____
_____
_____
_____
_____
_____
_____
_____
_____

The
reward of humility [and] the fear of the LORD
Are riches, honor and life.
Proverbs 22:4 (Read all of Proverbs 22)
New American Standard Bible

DEAR GOD,

_____
_____
_____
_____
_____
_____
_____
_____
_____
_____
_____
_____
_____
_____
_____
_____
_____
_____

With
[his] mouth the godless man destroys his
neighbor, But through knowledge the righteous
will be delivered.
Proverbs 11:9 (Read all of Proverbs 11)
New American Standard Bible

DEAR GOD,

_____
_____
_____
_____
_____
_____
_____
_____
_____
_____
_____
_____
_____
_____
_____
_____
_____
_____
_____

We love, because He first
loved us.
1 John 4:19 (Read all of 1 John 4)
New American Standard Bible

DEAR GOD,

_____
_____
_____
_____
_____
_____
_____
_____
_____
_____
_____
_____
_____
_____
_____
_____
_____
_____
_____

The wicked earns deceptive wages, But he who
sows righteousness [gets] a true reward.
Proverbs 11:18 (Read all of Proverbs 11)
New American Standard Bible

DEAR GOD,

_____
_____
_____
_____
_____
_____
_____
_____
_____
_____
_____
_____
_____
_____
_____
_____
_____
_____

May the Lord direct your hearts into the love
of God and into the steadfastness of Christ.
2 Thessalonians 3:5 (Read all of
2 Thessalonians 3)
New American Standard Bible

DEAR GOD,

Therefore you have no excuse, everyone of you
who passes judgment, for in that which you
judge another, you condemn yourself; for you
who judge practice the same things.
Romans 2:1 (Read all of Romans 2)
New American Standard Bible

DEAR GOD,

_____
_____
_____
_____
_____
_____
_____
_____
_____
_____
_____
_____
_____
_____
_____
_____
_____

Therefore, my beloved
brethren, be steadfast, immovable, always
abounding in the work of the Lord, knowing
that your toil is not [in] vain in the Lord.
1 Corinthians 15:58 (Read all of
1 Corinthians 15)
New American Standard Bible

DEAR GOD,

_____
_____
_____
_____
_____
_____
_____
_____
_____
_____
_____
_____
_____
_____
_____
_____
_____
_____

A fool does not delight in understanding, But
only in revealing his own mind.
Proverbs 18:2 (Read all of Proverbs 18)
New American Standard Bible

DEAR GOD,

_____

_____

_____

_____

_____

_____

_____

_____

_____

_____

_____

_____

_____

_____

_____

_____

_____

_____

_____

_____

But as for you, speak the things which are
fitting for sound doctrine.
Titus 2:1 (Read all of Titus 2)
New American Standard Bible

DEAR GOD,

_____
_____
_____
_____
_____
_____
_____
_____
_____
_____
_____
_____
_____

Your
adornment must not be [merely] external--
braiding the hair, and wearing gold jewelry,
or putting on dresses; God.
1 Peter 3:3 (Read all of 1 Peter 3)
New American Standard Bible

DEAR GOD,

_____
_____
_____
_____
_____
_____
_____
_____
_____
_____
_____
_____
_____
_____
_____
_____
_____

He said to me, "This is the
word of the LORD to Zerubbabel saying, 'Not
by might nor by power, but by My Spirit,'
says the LORD of hosts."
Zechariah 4:6 (Read all of Zechariah 4)
New American Standard Bible

DEAR GOD,

_____
_____
_____
_____
_____
_____
_____
_____
_____
_____
_____
_____
_____
_____
_____
_____

My soul thirsts for God, for the living God;
When shall I come and appear before God?
Psalm 42:2 (Read all of Psalm 42)
New American Standard Bible

DEAR GOD,

_____
_____
_____
_____
_____
_____
_____
_____
_____
_____
_____
_____
_____
_____
_____
_____
_____
_____
_____
_____

As for you, you meant evil
against me, [but] God meant it for good in
order to bring about this present result, to
preserve many people alive."
Genesis 50:20 (Read all of Genesis 50)
New American Standard Bible

DEAR GOD,

_____

_____

_____

_____

_____

_____

_____

_____

_____

_____

_____

_____

_____

_____

_____

After that He went out and noticed a tax
collector named Levi sitting in the tax
booth, and He said to him, "Follow Me."
Luke 5:27 (Read all of Luke 5)
New American Standard Bible

DEAR GOD,

_____
_____
_____
_____
_____
_____
_____
_____
_____
_____
_____
_____
_____
_____
_____
_____

But
the free gift is not like the transgression.
For if by the transgression of the one the
many died, much more did the grace of God and
the gift by the grace of the one Man, Jesus
Christ, abound to the many.
Romans 5:15 (Read all of Romans 5)
New American Standard Bible

DEAR GOD,

_____
_____
_____
_____
_____
_____
_____
_____
_____
_____
_____
_____
_____

But the free gift is not like the
transgression. For if by the transgression of
the one the many died, much more did the
grace of God and the gift by the grace of the
one Man, Jesus Christ, abound to the many.
Romans 5:15 (Read all of Romans 5)
New American Standard Bible

DEAR GOD,

_____
_____
_____
_____
_____
_____
_____
_____
_____
_____
_____
_____
_____
_____
_____
_____
_____

For
the whole Law is fulfilled in one word, in
the [statement,] "YOU SHALL LOVE YOUR
NEIGHBOR AS YOURSELF."
Galatians 5:14 (Read all of Galatians 5)
New American Standard Bible

DEAR GOD,

_____

_____

_____

_____

_____

_____

_____

_____

_____

_____

_____

_____

_____

_____

"The
fear of the LORD is to hate evil; Pride and
arrogance and the evil way And the perverted
mouth, I hate."
Proverbs 8:13 (Read all of Proverbs 8)
New American Standard Bible

DEAR GOD,

_____

_____

_____

_____

_____

_____

_____

_____

_____

_____

_____

_____

_____

_____

_____

_____

_____

_____

_____

_____

_____

For the mind set on the flesh is death, but
the mind set on the Spirit is life and peace,
Romans 8:6 (Read all of Romans 8)
New American Standard Bible

DEAR GOD,

_____
_____
_____
_____
_____
_____
_____
_____
_____
_____
_____
_____
_____
_____
_____
_____

As the deer pants for the water brooks, So my
soul pants for You, O God.
Psalm 42:1 (Read all of Psalm 42)
New American Standard Bible

DEAR GOD,

For a child will be born to us, a son will be given to us; And the government will rest on His shoulders; And His name will be called Wonderful Counselor, Mighty God, Eternal Father, Prince of Peace.
Isaiah 9:6 (Read all of Isaiah 9)
New American Standard Bible

DEAR GOD,

_____
_____
_____
_____
_____
_____
_____
_____
_____
_____
_____
_____
_____
_____
_____

By this we know that we abide in Him and He
in us, because He has given us of His Spirit.
1 John 4:13 (Read all of 1 John 4)
New American Standard Bible

DEAR GOD,

All discipline for the moment seems not to be joyful, but sorrowful; yet to those who have been trained by it, afterwards it yields the peaceful fruit of righteousness.
Hebrews 12:11 (Read all of Hebrews 12)
New American Standard Bible

DEAR GOD,

_____
_____
_____
_____
_____
_____
_____
_____
_____
_____
_____
_____
_____

"But
I do not consider my life of any account as
dear to myself, so that I may finish my
course and the ministry which I received from
the Lord Jesus, to testify solemnly of the
gospel of the grace of God."
Acts 20:24 (Read all of Acts 20)
New American Standard Bible

DEAR GOD,

_____
_____
_____
_____
_____
_____
_____
_____
_____
_____
_____
_____
_____
_____
_____
_____
_____
_____
_____
_____

"Then the mystery was revealed to Daniel in a
night vision. Then Daniel blessed the God of
heaven;
Daniel 2:19 (Read all of Daniel 2)
New American Standard Bible

DEAR GOD,

_____
_____
_____
_____
_____
_____
_____
_____
_____
_____
_____
_____
_____
_____
_____
_____
_____
_____

A fool rejects his father's discipline, But
he who regards reproof is sensible.
Proverbs 15:5 (Read all of Proverbs 15)
New American Standard Bible

DEAR GOD,

_____
_____
_____
_____
_____
_____
_____
_____
_____
_____
_____
_____
_____
_____
_____
_____

"But
you will receive power when the Holy Spirit
has come upon you; and you shall be My
witnesses both in Jerusalem, and in all Judea
and Samaria, and even to the remotest part of
the earth."
Acts 1:8 (Read all of Acts 1)
New American Standard Bible

DEAR GOD,

_____
_____
_____
_____
_____
_____
_____
_____
_____
_____
_____
_____
_____
_____
_____

I can do all things through Him who
strengthens me.
Philippians 4:13 (Read all of Philippians 4)
New American Standard Bible

DEAR GOD,

_____
_____
_____
_____
_____
_____
_____
_____
_____
_____
_____
_____
_____
_____
_____
_____
_____

Let no man deceive himself.
If any man among you thinks that he is wise
in this age, he must become foolish, so that
he may become wise.
1 Corinthians 3:18 (Read all of
1 Corinthians 3)
New American Standard Bible

DEAR GOD,

_____
_____
_____
_____
_____
_____
_____
_____
_____
_____
_____
_____
_____
_____

Now when Jesus came into the district of
Caesarea Philippi, He was asking His
disciples, "Who do people say that the Son of
Man is?"."
Matthew 16:13 (Read all of Matthew 16)
New American Standard Bible

DEAR GOD,

_____
_____
_____
_____
_____
_____
_____
_____
_____
_____
_____
_____
_____
_____
_____
_____
_____
_____
_____
_____

Through insolence comes nothing but strife,
But wisdom is with those who receive counsel.
Proverbs 13:10 (Read all of Proverbs 13)
New American Standard Bible

DEAR GOD,

_____

_____

_____

_____

_____

_____

_____

_____

_____

_____

_____

_____

_____

_____

For I determined to know nothing among you
except Jesus Christ, and Him crucified.
1 Corinthians 2:2 (Read all of
1 Corinthians 2)
New American Standard Bible

DEAR GOD,

_____
_____
_____
_____
_____
_____
_____
_____
_____
_____
_____
_____
_____
_____
_____
_____
_____
_____
_____
_____
_____

Create
in me a clean heart, O God, And renew a
steadfast spirit within me.
Psalm 51:10 (Read all of Psalm 51)
New American Standard Bible

DEAR GOD,

_____
_____
_____
_____
_____
_____
_____
_____
_____
_____
_____
_____
_____

Then this Daniel began distinguishing himself
among the commissioners and satraps because
he possessed an extraordinary spirit, and the
king planned to appoint him over the entire
kingdom.
Daniel 6:3 (Read all of Daniel 6)
New American Standard Bible

DEAR GOD,

He who loves money will not be satisfied with money, nor he who loves abundance [with its] income. This too is vanity.
Ecclesiastes 5:10 (Read all of Ecclesiastes 5)
New American Standard Bible

DEAR GOD,

_____

_____

_____

_____

_____

_____

_____

_____

_____

_____

_____

_____

From
the same mouth come [both] blessing and
cursing. My brethren, these things ought not
to be this way.
James 3:10 (Read all of James 3)
New American Standard Bible

DEAR GOD,

_____
_____
_____
_____
_____
_____
_____
_____
_____
_____
_____
_____
_____
_____
_____
_____
_____
_____

I will lift up my eyes to
the mountains; From where shall my help come?
Psalm 121:1 (Read all of Psalm 121)
New American Standard Bible

DEAR GOD,

_____

_____

_____

_____

_____

_____

_____

_____

_____

_____

_____

_____

_____

_____

_____

_____

There is no fear in love; but perfect love
casts out fear, because fear involves
punishment, and the one who fears is not
perfected in love.
1 John 4:18 (Read all of 1 John 4)
New American Standard Bible

DEAR GOD,

_____
_____
_____
_____
_____
_____
_____
_____
_____
_____
_____
_____
_____
_____
_____
_____
_____
_____

The mind of man plans his way, But the LORD
directs his steps.
Proverbs 16:9 (Read all of Proverbs 16)
New American Standard Bible

DEAR GOD,

_____
_____
_____
_____
_____
_____
_____
_____
_____
_____
_____
_____
_____
_____
_____
_____

"There is nothing covered up that will not be
revealed, and hidden that will not be known.
Luke 12:2 (Read all of Luke 12)
New American Standard Bible

DEAR GOD,

_____
_____
_____
_____
_____
_____
_____
_____
_____
_____
_____
_____
_____
_____
_____
_____
_____

Who will separate us from the love of Christ?
Will tribulation, or distress, or
persecution, or famine, or nakedness, or
peril, or sword? ....
Romans 8:35 (Read all of Romans 8)
New American Standard Bible

DEAR GOD,

_____
_____
_____
_____
_____
_____
_____
_____
_____
_____
_____
_____
_____
_____
_____
_____

His own iniquities will
capture the wicked, And he will be held with
the cords of his sin.
Proverbs 5:22 (Read all of Proverbs 5)
New American Standard Bible

DEAR GOD,

_____
_____
_____
_____
_____
_____
_____
_____
_____
_____
_____
_____
_____
_____
_____
_____
_____
_____

But godliness [actually] is
a means of great gain when accompanied by
contentment. For we have brought nothing into
the world, so we cannot take anything out of
it either.
1 Timothy 6:6-7 (Read all of 1 Timothy 6)
New American Standard Bible

DEAR GOD,

_____

_____

_____

_____

_____

_____

_____

_____

_____

_____

_____

_____

"When you pray, you are not to be like the
hypocrites; for they love to stand and pray
in the synagogues and on the street corners
so that they may be seen by men. Truly I say
to you, they have their reward in full.
Matthew 6:5 (Read all of Matthew 6)
New American Standard Bible

DEAR GOD,

_____

_____
_____
_____
_____
_____
_____
_____
_____
_____
_____
_____
_____
_____
_____
_____
_____
_____
_____

Therefore if there is any encouragement in
Christ, if there is any consolation of love,
if there is any fellowship of the Spirit, if
any affection and compassion,
Philippians 2:1 (Read all of Philippians 2)
New American Standard Bible

DEAR GOD,

_____

_____

_____

_____

_____

_____

_____

_____

_____

_____

_____

_____

_____

Stand firm therefore, HAVING GIRDED YOUR
LOINS WITH TRUTH, and HAVING PUT ON THE
BREASTPLATE OF RIGHTEOUSNESS,
Ephesians 6:14 (Read all of Ephesians 6)
New American Standard Bible

DEAR GOD,

_____
_____
_____
_____
_____
_____
_____
_____
_____
_____
_____
_____
_____
_____
_____
_____
_____
_____
_____
_____

Whoever confesses that Jesus is the Son of
God, God abides in him, and he in God.
1 John 4:15 (Read all of 1 John 4)
New American Standard Bible

DEAR GOD,

_____
_____
_____
_____
_____
_____
_____
_____
_____
_____
_____
_____
_____
_____
_____

The
grass withers, the flower fades, But the word
of our God stands forever.
Isaiah 40:8 (Read all of Isaiah 40)
New American Standard Bible

DEAR GOD,

_____
_____
_____
_____
_____
_____
_____
_____
_____
_____
_____
_____
_____
_____
_____
_____
_____
_____

After you have suffered for a little while,
the God of all grace, who called you to His
eternal glory in Christ, will Himself
perfect, confirm, strengthen [and] establish
you.
1 Peter 5:10 (Read all of 1 Peter 5)
New American Standard Bible

DEAR GOD,

_____

_____

_____

_____

_____

_____

_____

_____

_____

_____

_____

_____

_____

_____

And looking at [them] Jesus
said to them, "With people this is
impossible, but with God all things are
possible."
Matthew 19:26 (Read all of Matthew 19)
New American Standard Bible

DEAR GOD,

_____
_____
_____
_____
_____
_____
_____
_____
_____
_____
_____
_____
_____
_____
_____
_____
_____
_____
_____
_____

And without faith it is impossible to please
[Him,] for he who comes to God must believe
that He is and [that] He is a rewarder of
those who seek Him.
Hebrews 11:6 (Read all of Hebrews 11)
New American Standard Bible

DEAR GOD,

_____

_____

_____

_____

_____

_____

_____

_____

_____

_____

_____

_____

_____

_____

_____

So Joshua blessed
them and sent them and away, and they went
to their tents.
Joshua 22:6 (Read all of Joshua 22)
New American Standard Bible

DEAR GOD,

_____
_____
_____
_____
_____
_____
_____
_____
_____
_____
_____
_____
_____
_____
_____
_____
_____
_____

Do not
love the world nor the things in the world.
If anyone loves the world, the love of the
Father is not in him..
1 John 2:15 (Read all of 1 John 2)
New American Standard Bible

DEAR GOD,

_____
_____
_____
_____
_____
_____
_____
_____
_____
_____
_____
_____
_____
_____
_____
_____

If you do good to those who do good to you,
what credit is [that] to you? For even
sinners do the same."
Luke 6:33 (Read all of Luke 6)
New American Standard Bible

DEAR GOD,

_____

_____

_____

_____

_____

_____

_____

_____

_____

_____

_____

_____

_____

_____

_____

_____

_____

_____

Therefore, confess your sins to one another,
and pray for one another so that you may be
healed. The effective prayer of a righteous
man can accomplish much.
James 5:16 (Read all of James 5)
New American Standard Bible

DEAR GOD,

_____

_____

_____

_____

_____

_____

_____

_____

_____

_____

"Now, Israel, what does the LORD your God require from you, but to fear the LORD your God, to walk in all His ways and love Him, and toserve the LORD your God with all your heart and with all your soul,
Deuteronomy 10:12 (Read all of Deuteronomy 10)
New American Standard Bible

DEAR GOD,

_____
_____
_____
_____
_____
_____
_____
_____
_____
_____
_____
_____
_____
_____
_____
_____
_____
_____
_____

"He who believes in the Son has eternal life;
but he who does not obey the Son will not see
life, but the wrath of God abides on him."
John 3:36 (Read all of John 3)
New American Standard Bible

DEAR GOD,

_____
_____
_____
_____
_____
_____
_____
_____
_____
_____
_____
_____
_____
_____
_____

O taste and see that the LORD is good; How
blessed is the man who takes refuge in Him!
Psalm 34:8 (Read all of Psalm 34)
New American Standard Bible

DEAR GOD,

_____
_____
_____
_____
_____
_____
_____
_____
_____
_____
_____
_____
_____
_____
_____
_____
_____
_____
_____

For as through the one man's
disobedience the many were made sinners, even
so through the obedience of the One the many
will be made righteous.
Romans 5:19 (Read all of Romans 5)
New American Standard Bible

DEAR GOD,

_____

_____

_____

_____

_____

_____

_____

_____

_____

_____

_____

_____

_____

_____

_____

I would have despaired] unless I had believed
that I would see the goodness of the LORD In
the land of the living.
Psalm 27:13 (Read all of Psalm 27)
New American Standard Bible

DEAR GOD,

_____
_____
_____
_____
_____
_____
_____
_____
_____
_____
_____
_____
_____
_____
_____
_____
_____
_____
_____

The one who does not
love does not know God, for God is love.
1 John 4:8 (Read all of 1 John 4)
New American Standard Bible

DEAR GOD,

_____

_____

_____

_____

_____

_____

_____

_____

_____

_____

_____

_____

_____

_____

_____

Rejoice in the Lord; again I will say,
rejoice
Philippians 4:4 (Read all of
Philippians 3)
New American Standard Bible

DEAR GOD,

Go to the ant, O sluggard, Observe her ways
and be wise,
Proverbs 6:6 (Read all of Proverbs 6)
New American Standard Bible

DEAR GOD,

_____
_____
_____
_____
_____
_____
_____
_____
_____
_____
_____
_____
_____
_____
_____
_____

Do not be wise in your own eyes; Fear the
LORD and turn away from evil.
Proverbs 3:7 (Read all of Proverbs 3)
New American Standard Bible

DEAR GOD,

With it we bless [our] Lord and Father, and
with it we curse men, who have been made in
the likeness of God;
James 3:9 (Read all of James 3)
New American Standard Bible

DEAR GOD,

_____

_____

_____

_____

_____

_____

_____

_____

_____

_____

_____

_____

_____

"I am the LORD, that is My name; I will not
give My glory to another, Nor My praise to
graven images."
Isaiah 42:8 (Read all of Isaiah 42)
New American Standard Bible

DEAR GOD,

_____
_____
_____
_____
_____
_____
_____
_____
_____
_____
_____
_____
_____
_____
_____
_____
_____
_____
_____
_____
_____

For the mind set on the flesh is death, but
the mind set on the Spirit is life and peace.
Romans 8:6 (Read all of Romans 8)
New American Standard Bible

DEAR GOD,

_____

_____

_____

_____

_____

_____

_____

_____

_____

_____

_____

_____

_____

_____

"Blessed are those who have been persecuted
for the sake of righteousness, for theirs is
the kingdom of heaven."
Matthew 5:10 (Read all of Matthew 5)
New American Standard Bible

DEAR GOD,

_____
_____
_____
_____
_____
_____
_____
_____
_____
_____
_____
_____
_____
_____
_____
_____
_____
_____
_____

Seek the LORD and His strength; Seek His face
continually.
1 Chronicles 16:11-12 (Read all of
1 Chronicles 16)
New American Standard Bible

DEAR GOD,

_____

_____

_____

_____

_____

_____

_____

_____

_____

_____

_____

_____

_____

_____

_____

_____

Hear, O LORD, when I cry with my voice,
Psalm 27:7, (Read all of Psalm 27)
New American Standard Bible

DEAR GOD,

_____
_____
_____
_____
_____
_____
_____
_____
_____
_____
_____
_____
_____
_____
_____
_____
_____
_____

Above all, keep fervent in your love for one
another, because love covers a multitude of
sins.
1 Peter 4:8 (Read all of 1 Peter 4)
New American Standard Bible

DEAR GOD,

_____
_____
_____
_____
_____
_____
_____
_____
_____
_____
_____
_____
_____
_____
_____
_____
_____
_____

Every man's way is right in his own eyes, But
the LORD weighs the hearts.
Proverbs 21:2 (Read all of Proverbs 21)
New American Standard Bible

DEAR GOD,

_____
_____
_____
_____
_____
_____
_____
_____
_____
_____
_____
_____
_____
_____
_____
_____
_____
_____
_____
_____
_____
_____
_____

Why are you in despair, O my soul? And why
have you become disturbed within me? Hope in
God, for I shall yet praise Him, The help of
my countenance and my God.
Psalm 42:11 (Read all of Psalm 42)
New American Standard Bible

DEAR GOD,

_____

_____

_____

_____

_____

_____

_____

_____

_____

_____

_____

_____

And he answered, "YOU SHALL LOVE THE LORD
YOUR GOD WITH ALL YOUR HEART, AND WITH ALL
YOUR SOUL, AND WITH ALL YOUR STRENGTH, AND
WITH ALL YOUR MIND; AND YOUR NEIGHBOR AS
YOURSELF."
Luke 10:27 (Read all of Luke 10)
New American Standard Bible

DEAR GOD,

_____
_____
_____
_____
_____
_____
_____
_____
_____
_____
_____
_____
_____
_____
_____
_____
_____
_____
_____
_____

God is love, and the one who abides in love
abides in God, and God abides in him.
1 John 4:16b (Read all of 1 John 4)
New American Standard Bible

DEAR GOD,

_____

_____

_____

_____

_____

_____

_____

_____

_____

_____

_____

_____

_____

_____

For in Christ Jesus neither circumcision nor
uncircumcision means anything, but faith
working through love.
Galatians 5:6 (Read all of Galatians 5)
New American Standard Bible

DEAR GOD,

_____
_____
_____
_____
_____
_____
_____
_____
_____
_____
_____
_____
_____
_____
_____
_____

But sanctify Christ as Lord in your hearts,
always [being] ready to make a defense to
everyone who asks you to give an account for
the hope that is in you, yet with gentleness
and reverence.
1 Peter 3:15 (Read all of 1 Peter 3)
New American Standard Bible

DEAR GOD,

_____

_____

_____

_____

_____

_____

_____

_____

_____

_____

_____

_____

_____

_____

_____

_____

"Do not judge so that you will not be
judged."
Matthew 7:1 (Read all of Matthew 7)
New American Standard Bible

DEAR GOD,

_____
_____
_____
_____
_____
_____
_____
_____
_____
_____
_____
_____
_____
_____
_____
_____
_____
_____

"Let it be known to all of you and to all the people of Israel, that by the name of Jesus Christ the Nazarene, whom you crucified, whom God raised from the dead--by this [name] this man stands here before you in good health.
Acts 4:10 (Read all of Acts 4)
New American Standard Bible

DEAR GOD,

_____

_____

_____

_____

_____

_____

_____

_____

_____

_____

_____

_____

_____

_____

But as many as received Him, to them He gave
the right to become children of God, [even]
to those who believe in His name,
John 1:12-1 (Read all of John 1)
New American Standard Bible

DEAR GOD,

_____
_____
_____
_____
_____
_____
_____
_____
_____
_____
_____
_____
_____
_____
_____
_____
_____
_____

If, however, you are fulfilling the royal law
according to the Scripture, "YOU SHALL LOVE
YOUR NEIGHBOR AS YOURSELF," you are doing
well.
James 2:8 (Read all of James 2)
New American Standard Bible

DEAR GOD,

Therefore what benefit were you then deriving
from the things of which you are now ashamed?
For the outcome of those things is death.
Romans 6:21 (Read all of Romans 6)
New American Standard Bible

DEAR GOD,

_____
_____
_____
_____
_____
_____
_____
_____
_____
_____
_____
_____
_____
_____
_____

See that no one repays another with evil for evil, but always seek after that which is good for one another and for all people.
1 Thessalonians 5:15 (Read all of
1 Thessalonians 5)
New American Standard Bible

DEAR GOD,

Behold, the eye of the LORD is on those who
fear Him, On those who hope for His
lovingkindness.
Psalm 33:18 (Read all of Psalm 33)
New American Standard Bible

DEAR GOD,

_____
_____
_____
_____
_____
_____
_____
_____
_____
_____
_____
_____
_____
_____
_____
_____
_____
_____
_____
_____
_____

Whoever believes that Jesus is the Christ is
born of God, and whoever loves the Father
loves the [child] born of Him.
1 John 5:1 (Read all of 1 John 5)
New American Standard Bible

DEAR GOD,

_____
_____
_____
_____
_____
_____
_____
_____
_____
_____
_____
_____
_____
_____
_____

"He who believes in Him is not judged; he who
does not believe has been judged already,
because he has not believed in the name of
the only begotten Son of God."
John 3:18 (Read all of John 3)
New American Standard Bible

DEAR GOD,

_____
_____
_____
_____
_____
_____
_____
_____
_____
_____
_____
_____
_____
_____
_____
_____
_____
_____
_____
_____
_____
_____

Hatred stirs up strife, But love covers all
transgressions.
Proverbs 10:12 (Read all of Proverbs 10)
New American Standard Bible

DEAR GOD,

_____
_____
_____
_____
_____
_____
_____
_____
_____
_____
_____
_____
_____
_____
_____

Because by the works of the Law no flesh will
be justified in His sight; for through the
Law [comes] the knowledge of sin.
Romans 3:20 (Read all of Romans 3)
New American Standard Bible

DEAR GOD,

_____
_____
_____
_____
_____
_____
_____
_____
_____
_____
_____
_____
_____
_____
_____
_____
_____
_____
_____
_____
_____

righteousness to everyone who believes.
Romans 10:4 (Read all of Romans 10)
New American Standard Bible

DEAR GOD,

_____

_____

_____

_____

_____

_____

_____

_____

_____

_____

_____

_____

_____

Beloved, do not be surprised at the fiery
ordeal among you, which comes upon you for
your testing, as though some strange thing
were happening to you;.
1 Peter 4:12 (Read all of 1 Peter 4)
New American Standard Bible

DEAR GOD,

_____
_____
_____
_____
_____
_____
_____
_____
_____
_____
_____
_____
_____
_____
_____
_____
_____
_____
_____

"Because he has loved Me, therefore I will
deliver him; I will set him [securely] on
high, because he has known My name."
Psalm 91:14 (Read all of Psalm 91)
New American Standard Bible

DEAR GOD,

_____

_____

_____

_____

_____

_____

_____

_____

_____

_____

_____

_____

_____

_____

_____

_____

And the seed whose fruit is righteousness is
sown in peace by those who make peace.
James 3:18 (Read all of James 3)
New American Standard Bible

DEAR GOD,

_____
_____
_____
_____
_____
_____
_____
_____
_____
_____
_____
_____
_____
_____
_____
_____
_____
_____

"But I say to you, love your enemies and pray
for those who persecute you, ...
Matthew 5:44 (Read all of Matthew 5)
New American Standard Bible

DEAR GOD,

_____
_____
_____
_____
_____
_____
_____
_____
_____
_____
_____
_____
_____
_____
_____
_____

But Jesus turning and seeing her said,
"Daughter, take courage; your faith has made
you well." At once the woman was made well.
Matthew 9:22 (Read all of Matthew 9)
New American Standard Bible

DEAR GOD,

_____
_____
_____
_____
_____
_____
_____
_____
_____
_____
_____
_____
_____
_____
_____
_____
_____
_____
_____

"Do not store up for yourselves treasures on
earth, where moth and rust destroy, and where
thieves break in and steal.
Matthew 6:19 (Read all of Matthew 6)
New American Standard Bible

DEAR GOD,

_____

_____

_____

_____

_____

_____

_____

_____

_____

_____

_____

_____

_____

Jesus Christ gave Himself for us to redeem us
from every lawless deed, and to purify for
Himself a people for His own possession,
zealous for good deeds.
Titus 2:14 (Read all of Titus 2)
New American Standard Bible

DEAR GOD,

"Now I, Nebuchadnezzar, praise, exalt and honor the King of heaven, for all His works are true and His ways just, and He is able to humble those who walk in pride."
Daniel 4:37 (Read all of Daniel 4)
New American Standard Bible

DEAR GOD,

_____

_____

_____

_____

_____

_____

_____

_____

_____

_____

_____

_____

Therefore, putting aside all filthiness and
[all] that remains of wickedness, in humility
receive the word implanted, which is able to
save your souls.
James 1:21 (Read all of James 1)
New American Standard Bible

DEAR GOD,

_____
_____
_____
_____
_____
_____
_____
_____
_____
_____
_____
_____
_____
_____
_____
_____
_____
_____
_____
_____
_____
_____

Wise men store up knowledge, But with the
mouth of the foolish, ruin is at hand.
Proverbs 10:14 (Read all of Proverbs 10)
New American Standard Bible

DEAR GOD,

_____
_____
_____
_____
_____
_____
_____
_____
_____
_____
_____
_____

One thing I have asked from the LORD, that I
shall seek: That I may dwell in the house of
the LORD all the days of my life, To behold
the beauty of the LORD And to meditate in His
temple.
Psalm 27:4 (Read all of Psalm 27)
New American Standard Bible

DEAR GOD,

_____

_____

_____

_____

_____

_____

_____

_____

_____

_____

_____

_____

_____

_____

_____

_____

_____

_____

Therefore, having been justified by faith, we
have peace with God through our Lord Jesus
Christ,
Romans 5:1- (Read all of Romans 5)
New American Standard Bible

DEAR GOD,

_____

_____

_____

_____

_____

_____

_____

_____

_____

_____

_____

"All the commandments that I am commanding
you today you shall be careful to do, that
you may live and multiply, and go in and
possess the land which the LORD swore [to
give] to your forefathers.
Deuteronomy 8:1 (Read all of Deuteronomy 8)
New American Standard Bible

DEAR GOD,

_____
_____
_____
_____
_____
_____
_____
_____
_____
_____
_____
_____
_____
_____
_____
_____
_____
_____
_____
_____

Behold, how good and how pleasant it is For
brothers to dwell together in unity!
Psalm 133:1 (Read all of Psalm 133)
New American Standard Bible

DEAR GOD,

_____

_____

_____

_____

_____

_____

_____

_____

_____

_____

_____

_____

_____

_____

_____

How blessed are those whose way is blameless,
Who walk in the law of the LORD..
Psalm 119:1 (Read all of Psalm 119)
New American Standard Bible

DEAR GOD,

My mouth is filled with Your praise And with
Your glory all day long.
Psalm 71:8 (Read all of Psalm 71)
New American Standard Bible

DEAR GOD,

_____
_____
_____
_____
_____
_____
_____
_____
_____
_____
_____
_____
_____
_____
_____
_____

"Blessed are those who hunger and thirst for
righteousness, for they shall be satisfied."
Matthew 5:6 (Read all of Matthew 5)
New American Standard Bible

DEAR GOD,

_____
_____
_____
_____
_____
_____
_____
_____
_____
_____
_____
_____
_____
_____
_____
_____
_____
_____

Therefore humble yourselves under the mighty
hand of God, that He may exalt you at the
proper time.
1 Peter 5:6 (Read all of 1 Peter 5)
New American Standard Bible

DEAR GOD,

_____

_____

_____

_____

_____

_____

_____

_____

_____

_____

_____

_____

_____

_____

_____

_____

Do not be overcome by evil, but overcome evil
with good.
Romans 12:21 (Read all of Romans 12)
New American Standard Bible

DEAR GOD,

_____
_____
_____
_____
_____
_____
_____
_____
_____
_____
_____
_____
_____
_____
_____
_____
_____
_____
_____
_____
_____
_____
_____

"Therefore be on the alert, for you do not
know which day your Lord is coming.
Matthew 24:42 (Read all of Matthew 24)
New American Standard Bible

DEAR GOD,

_____
_____
_____
_____
_____
_____
_____
_____
_____
_____
_____
_____
_____
_____
_____

[Let] love [be] without hypocrisy. Abhor what
is evil; cling to what is good..
Romans 12:9 (Read all of Romans 12)
New American Standard Bible

DEAR GOD,

_____
_____
_____
_____
_____
_____
_____
_____
_____
_____
_____
_____
_____
_____
_____
_____

But God has chosen the
foolish things of the world to shame the
wise, and God has chosen the weak things of
the world to shame the things which are
strong,
1 Corinthians 1:27 (Read all of
1 Corinthians 1)
New American Standard Bible

DEAR GOD,

_____

_____

_____

_____

_____

_____

_____

_____

_____

_____

_____

_____

_____

_____

When there are many words, transgression is
unavoidable, But he who restrains his lips is
wise.
Proverbs 10:19 (Read all of Proverbs 10)
New American Standard Bible

DEAR GOD,

_____
_____
_____
_____
_____
_____
_____
_____
_____
_____
_____
_____
_____
_____
_____
_____
_____

"For My people have committed two evils: They
have forsaken Me, The fountain of living
waters, To hew for themselves cisterns,
Broken cisterns That can hold no water."
Jeremiah 2:13 (Read all of Jeremiah 2)
New American Standard Bible

DEAR GOD,

_____
_____
_____
_____
_____
_____
_____
_____
_____
_____
_____
_____
_____
_____
_____

My son, do not reject the discipline of the
LORD Or loathe His reproof,
Proverbs 3:11 (Read all of Proverbs 3)
New American Standard Bible

DEAR GOD,

Do not be deceived, God is not mocked; for whatever a man sows, this he will also reap. Galatians 6:7(Read all of Galatians 6) New American Standard Bible

DEAR GOD,

_____
_____
_____
_____
_____
_____
_____
_____
_____
_____
_____
_____
_____
_____
_____
_____
_____

I stretch out my hands to You; My soul
[longs] for You, as a parched land.
Psalm 143:6 (Read all of Psalm 143)
New American Standard Bible

DEAR GOD,

_____
_____
_____
_____
_____
_____
_____
_____
_____
_____
_____
_____
_____
_____
_____
_____
_____
_____
_____
_____
_____
_____
_____

"Those who regard vain idols Forsake their
faithfulness."
Jonah 2:8 (Read all of Jonah 2)
New American Standard Bible

DEAR GOD,

_____
_____
_____
_____
_____
_____
_____
_____
_____
_____
_____
_____
_____
_____
_____

"But go and learn what this means: 'I DESIRE
COMPASSION, AND NOT SACRIFICE,' for I did not
come to call the righteous, but sinners."
Matthew 9:13 (Read all of Matthew 9)
New American Standard Bible

DEAR GOD,

_____
_____
_____
_____
_____
_____
_____
_____
_____
_____
_____
_____
_____
_____
_____
_____

"I call heaven and earth to witness against
you today, that I have set before you life
and death, the blessing and the curse. So
choose life in order that you may live, you
and your descendants."
Deuteronomy 30:19 (Read all of
Deuteronomy 30)
New American Standard Bible

DEAR GOD,

_____
_____
_____
_____
_____
_____
_____
_____
_____
_____
_____
_____
_____
_____
_____
_____

[Like] a city that is broken into [and]
without walls Is a man who has no control
over his spirit.
Proverbs 25:28 (Read all of Proverbs 25)
New American Standard Bible

DEAR GOD,

_____

_____

_____

_____

_____

_____

_____

_____

_____

_____

_____

_____

_____

_____

_____

_____

_____

_____

_____

_____

Remember, O LORD, Your compassion and Your
lovingkindnesses, For they have been from of
old.
Psalm 25:6 (Read all of Psalm 25)
New American Standard Bible

DEAR GOD,

_____
_____
_____
_____
_____
_____
_____
_____
_____
_____
_____
_____
_____
_____
_____
_____
_____

A man's pride will bring him low, But a
humble spirit will obtain honor.
Proverbs 29:23 (Read all of Proverbs 29)
New American Standard Bible

DEAR GOD,

_____
_____
_____
_____
_____
_____
_____
_____
_____
_____
_____
_____
_____
_____
_____
_____
_____
_____
_____
_____

I passed by the field of the sluggard And by
the vineyard of the man lacking sense,
Proverbs 24:30 (Read all of Proverbs 24)
New American Standard Bible

DEAR GOD,

_____

_____

_____

_____

_____

_____

_____

_____

_____

_____

_____

_____

_____

For I am not ashamed of the gospel, for it is
the power of God for salvation to everyone
who believes, to the Jew first and also to
the Greek.
Romans 1:16 (Read all of Romans 1)
New American Standard Bible

DEAR GOD,

_____

_____

_____

_____

_____

_____

_____

_____

_____

_____

_____

_____

_____

_____

_____

_____

_____

_____

_____

John testified saying, "I have seen the
Spirit descending as a dove out of heaven,
and He remained upon Him. "I did not
recognize Him,
John 1:32-34 (Read all of John 1)
New American Standard Bible

DEAR GOD,

_____
_____
_____
_____
_____
_____
_____
_____
_____
_____
_____
_____
_____
_____
_____

But when they saw Him walking on the sea,
They supposed that it was a ghost, and cried
out;
Mark 6:49 (Read all of Mark 6)
New American Standard Bible

DEAR GOD,

_____
_____
_____
_____
_____
_____
_____
_____
_____
_____
_____
_____
_____
_____
_____
_____
_____
_____
_____
_____
_____
_____

But He said, "The things that are impossible
with people are possible with God."
Luke 18:27 (Read all of Luke 18)
New American Standard Bible

DEAR GOD,

_____
_____
_____
_____
_____
_____
_____
_____
_____
_____
_____
_____
_____
_____
_____

Let us not lose heart in doing good, for in
due time we will reap if we do not grow
weary.
Galatians 6:9 (Read all of Galatians 6)
New American Standard Bible

DEAR GOD,

_____
_____
_____
_____
_____
_____
_____
_____
_____
_____
_____
_____
_____
_____
_____
_____
_____
_____
_____
_____
_____

"Blessed is the man who trusts in the LORD
And whose trust is the LORD."
Jeremiah 17:7 (Read all of Jeremiah 17)
New American Standard Bible

DEAR GOD,

_____

_____

_____

_____

_____

_____

_____

_____

_____

_____

_____

_____

_____

_____

_____

"For this reason You are great, O Lord GOD;
for there is none like You, and there is no
God besides You."
2 Samuel 7:22 (Read all of 2 Samuel 7)
New American Standard Bible

DEAR GOD,

_____
_____
_____
_____
_____
_____
_____
_____
_____
_____
_____
_____
_____
_____
_____
_____
_____

How blessed is the man who does not walk in
the counsel of the wicked, Nor stand in the
path of sinners, Nor sit in the seat of
scoffers!
Psalm 1:1 (Read all of Psalm 1)
New American Standard Bible

DEAR GOD,

_____

_____

_____

_____

_____

_____

_____

_____

_____

_____

_____

_____

_____

_____

For this is the message which you have heard
from the beginning, that we should love one
another.
1 John 3:11 (Read all of 1 John 3)
New American Standard Bible

DEAR GOD,

_____
_____
_____
_____
_____
_____
_____
_____
_____
_____
_____
_____
_____
_____
_____
_____
_____
_____
_____
_____
_____
_____
_____
_____

When pride comes, then comes dishonor, But
with the humble is wisdom.
Proverbs 11:2 (Read all of Proverbs 11)
New American Standard Bible

DEAR GOD,

_____
_____
_____
_____
_____
_____
_____
_____
_____
_____
_____
_____
_____
_____
_____
_____
_____
_____
_____

Jesus said to him, "I am the way, and the
truth, and the life; no one comes to the
Father but through Me."
John 14:6 (Read all of John 14)
New American Standard Bible

DEAR GOD,

"For this commandment which I command you
today is not too difficult for you, nor is it
out of reach.
Deuteronomy 30:11 (Read all of
Deuteronomy 30)
New American Standard Bible

DEAR GOD,

_____
_____
_____
_____
_____
_____
_____
_____
_____
_____
_____
_____
_____
_____
_____
_____

Death and life are in the power of the
tongue, And those who love it will eat its
fruit.
Proverbs 18:21 (Read all of Proverbs 18)
New American Standard Bible

DEAR GOD,

_____
_____
_____
_____
_____
_____
_____
_____
_____
_____
_____
_____
_____
_____
_____
_____

"This is My commandment, that you love one
another, just as I have loved you. Greater
love has no one than this, that one lay down
his life for his friends."
John 15:12-13 (Read all of John 15)
New American Standard Bible

DEAR GOD,

_____
_____
_____
_____
_____
_____
_____
_____
_____
_____
_____
_____
_____
_____

You adulteresses, do you not know that
friendship with the world is hostility toward
God? Therefore whoever wishes to be a friend
of the world makes himself an enemy of God.
James 4:4 (Read all of James 4)
New American Standard Bible

DEAR GOD,

_____
_____
_____
_____
_____
_____
_____
_____
_____
_____
_____
_____
_____
_____
_____
_____
_____
_____
_____

He who is slow to anger is better than the
mighty, And he who rules his spirit, than he
who captures a city.
Proverbs 16:32 (Read all of Proverbs 16)
New American Standard Bible

DEAR GOD,

_____
_____
_____
_____
_____
_____
_____
_____
_____
_____
_____
_____
_____
_____
_____
_____
_____

There is a way [which seems] right to a man,
But its end is the way of death.
Proverbs 16:25 (Read all of Proverbs 16)
New American Standard Bible

DEAR GOD,

_____
_____
_____
_____
_____
_____
_____
_____
_____
_____
_____
_____
_____
_____
_____
_____
_____
_____

It is a trustworthy statement, deserving full
acceptance, that Christ Jesus came into the
world to save sinners, among whom I am
foremost [of all.]
1 Timothy 1:15 (Read all of 1 Timothy 1)
New American Standard Bible

DEAR GOD,

_____
_____
_____
_____
_____
_____
_____
_____
_____
_____
_____
_____
_____
_____
_____
_____

"But now I come to You; and these things I
speak in the world so that they may have My
joy made full in themselves."
John 17:13 (Read all of John 17)
New American Standard Bible

DEAR GOD,

Now I urge you, brethren, keep your eye on
those who cause dissensions and hindrances
contrary to the teaching which you learned,
and turn away from them.
Romans 16:17 (Read all of Romans 16)
New American Standard Bible

DEAR GOD,

_____

_____

_____

_____

_____

_____

_____

_____

_____

_____

_____

_____

_____

_____

He has told you, O man, what is good; And
what does the LORD require of you But to do
justice, to love kindness, And to walk humbly
with your God?
Micah 6:8 (Read all of Micah 6)
New American Standard Bible

DEAR GOD,

_____
_____
_____
_____
_____
_____
_____
_____
_____
_____
_____
_____
_____
_____
_____
_____
_____
_____
_____
_____

And Jesus [continued] by questioning them,
"But who do you say that I am?" Peter
answered and said to Him, "You are the
Christ."
Mark 8:29 (Read all of Mark 8)
New American Standard Bible

DEAR GOD,

"Beware of the false prophets, who come to
you in sheep's clothing, but inwardly are
ravenous wolves."
Matthew 7:15 (Read all of Matthew 7)
New American Standard Bible

DEAR GOD,

_____
_____
_____
_____
_____
_____
_____
_____
_____
_____
_____
_____
_____
_____
_____
_____
_____
_____

"For there is no good tree which produces bad
fruit, nor, on the other hand, a bad tree
which produces good fruit.
Luke 6:43 (Read all of Luke 6)
New American Standard Bible

DEAR GOD,

_____

_____

_____

_____

_____

_____

_____

_____

_____

_____

_____

_____

_____

By faith even Sarah herself
received ability to conceive, even beyond the
proper time of life, since she considered Him
faithful who had promised.
Hebrews 11:11 (Read all of Hebrews 11)
New American Standard Bible

DEAR GOD,

_____
_____
_____
_____
_____
_____
_____
_____
_____
_____
_____
_____
_____
_____
_____
_____
_____
_____

And though you have not seen Him, you love
Him, and though you do not see Him now, but
believe in Him, you greatly rejoice with joy
inexpressible and full of glory, o
1 Peter 1:8 (Read all of 1 Peter 1)
New American Standard Bible

DEAR GOD,

_____
_____
_____
_____
_____
_____
_____
_____
_____
_____
_____
_____
_____
_____

In this is love, not that we loved God, but
that He loved us and sent His Son [to be] the
propitiation for our sins.
1 John 4:10 (Read all of 1 John 4)
New American Standard Bible

DEAR GOD,

_____
_____
_____
_____
_____
_____
_____
_____
_____
_____
_____
_____
_____
_____
_____
_____
_____
_____
_____

A soothing tongue is a tree of life, But
perversion in it crushes the spirit.
Proverbs 15:4 (Read all of Proverbs 15)
New American Standard Bible

DEAR GOD,

_____
_____
_____
_____
_____
_____
_____
_____
_____
_____
_____
_____
_____
_____
_____
_____

Jesus answered and said to them, "This is the work of God, that you believe in Him whom He has sent."
John 6:29 (Read all of John 6)
New American Standard Bible

DEAR GOD,

_____
_____
_____
_____
_____
_____
_____
_____
_____
_____
_____
_____
_____
_____
_____
_____
_____
_____
_____

Do not be bound together with unbelievers;
for what partnership have righteousness and
lawlessness, or what fellowship has light
with darkness?
2 Corinthians 6:14 (Read all of
2 Corinthians 6)
New American Standard Bible

DEAR GOD,

_____
_____
_____
_____
_____
_____
_____
_____
_____
_____
_____
_____

for bodily discipline is only of little
profit, but godliness is profitable for all
things, since it holds promise for the
present life and [also] for the [life] to
come.
1 Timothy 4:8 (Read all of 1 Timothy 4)
New American Standard Bible

DEAR GOD,

Beloved, do not believe every spirit, but
test the spirits to see whether they are from
God, because many false prophets have gone
out into the world.
1 John 4:1 (Read all of 1 John 4)
New American Standard Bible

DEAR GOD,

_____
_____
_____
_____
_____
_____
_____
_____
_____
_____
_____
_____
_____
_____
_____
_____

AND YOU SHALL LOVE THE LORD YOUR GOD WITH ALL
YOUR HEART, AND WITH ALL YOUR SOUL, AND WITH
ALL YOUR MIND, AND WITH ALL YOUR STRENGTH.
Mark 12:30 (Read all of Mark 12)
New American Standard Bible

DEAR GOD,

_____
_____
_____
_____
_____
_____
_____
_____
_____
_____
_____
_____
_____
_____
_____
_____
_____
_____
_____
_____
_____
_____

The fear of the LORD is the instruction for
wisdom, And before honor [comes] humility.
Proverbs 15:33 (Read all of Proverbs 15)
New American Standard Bible

DEAR GOD,

_____

_____

_____

_____

_____

_____

_____

_____

_____

_____

_____

_____

_____

_____

How
lovely on the mountains Are the feet of him
who brings good news, Who announces peace And
brings good news of happiness, Who announces
salvation, [And] says to Zion, "Your God
reigns!"
Isaiah 52:7 (Read all of Isaiah 52)
New American Standard Bible

DEAR GOD,

_____

_____

_____

_____

_____

_____

_____

_____

_____

_____

_____

_____

_____

_____

_____

_____

He who dwells in the shelter of the Most High
Will abide in the shadow of the Almighty.
Psalm 91:1 (Read all of Psalm 91)
New American Standard Bible

DEAR GOD,

_____
_____
_____
_____
_____
_____
_____
_____
_____
_____
_____
_____
_____
_____
_____

"Had it not been the LORD who was on our side
When men rose up against us,;
Psalm 124:2 (Read all of Psalm 124)
New American Standard Bible

DEAR GOD,

But now apart from the Law [the]
righteousness of God has been manifested,
being witnessed by the Law and the Prophets,
Romans 3:21 (Read all of Romans 3)
New American Standard Bible

DEAR GOD,

_____

_____

_____

_____

_____

_____

_____

_____

_____

_____

_____

_____

_____

_____

_____

For to you it has been granted for Christ's sake, not only to believe in Him, but also to suffer for His sake.
Philippians 1:29 (Read all of Philippians 1)
New American Standard Bible

DEAR GOD,

_____
_____
_____
_____
_____
_____
_____
_____
_____
_____
_____
_____
_____
_____
_____
_____
_____
_____
_____

For we are His workmanship, created in Christ
Jesus for good works, which God prepared
beforehand so that we would walk in them.
Ephesians 2:10 (Read all of Ephesians 2)
New American Standard Bible

DEAR GOD,

_____
_____
_____
_____
_____
_____
_____
_____
_____
_____
_____
_____
_____
_____
_____
_____

Do not participate in the unfruitful deeds of
darkness, but instead even expose them;
Ephesians 5:11 (Read all of Ephesians 5)
New American Standard Bible

DEAR GOD,

_____
_____
_____
_____
_____
_____
_____
_____
_____
_____
_____
_____
_____
_____
_____
_____
_____
_____
_____
_____
_____

Fathers, do not provoke your children to
anger, but bring them up in the discipline
and instruction of the Lord.
Ephesians 6:4 (Read all of Ephesians 6)
New American Standard Bible

DEAR GOD,

_____
_____
_____
_____
_____
_____
_____
_____
_____
_____
_____
_____
_____
_____

The people answered and said, "Far be it from
Us that we should forsake the LORD to serve
Other gods;
Joshua 24:16 (Read all of Joshua 24)
New American Standard Bible

DEAR GOD,

_____
_____
_____
_____
_____
_____
_____
_____
_____
_____
_____
_____
_____
_____
_____
_____
_____
_____
_____
_____
_____

Little children, guard yourselves from idols.
1 John 5:21 (Read all of 1 John 5)
New American Standard Bible

DEAR GOD,

_____

_____

_____

_____

_____

_____

_____

_____

_____

_____

_____

_____

_____

Indeed, [while following] the way of Your
judgments, O LORD, We have waited for You
eagerly; Your name, even Your memory, is the
desire of [our] souls.
Isaiah 26:8 (Read all of Isaiah 26)
New American Standard Bible

DEAR GOD,

_____
_____
_____
_____
_____
_____
_____
_____
_____
_____
_____
_____
_____
_____
_____
_____
_____
_____
_____
_____
_____
_____
_____
_____

But prove yourselves doers of the word, and
not merely hearers who delude themselves.
James 1:22 (Read all of James 1)
New American Standard Bible

DEAR GOD,

_____
_____
_____
_____
_____
_____
_____
_____
_____
_____
_____
_____
_____

We know that God causes all
things to work together for good to those who
love God, to those who are called according
to [His] purpose.
Romans 8:28 (Read all of Romans 8)
New American Standard Bible

DEAR GOD,

_____
_____
_____
_____
_____
_____
_____
_____
_____
_____
_____
_____
_____
_____
_____
_____
_____
_____
_____
_____
_____

Be gracious to me, O God, according to Your
lovingkindness; According to the greatness of
Your compassion blot out my transgressions.
Psalm 51:1 (Read all of Psalm 51)
New American Standard Bible

DEAR GOD,

_____
_____
_____
_____
_____
_____
_____
_____
_____
_____
_____
_____
_____
_____

But I say, walk by the Spirit, and you will
not carry out the desire of the flesh.
Galatians 5:16 (Read all of Galatians 5)
New American Standard Bible

DEAR GOD,

_____
_____
_____
_____
_____
_____
_____
_____
_____
_____
_____
_____
_____
_____
_____
_____
_____

Therefore be imitators of God, as beloved

children;
Ephesians 5:1-2 (Read all of Ephesians 5)
New American Standard Bible

DEAR GOD,

_____
_____
_____
_____
_____
_____
_____
_____
_____
_____
_____
_____
_____
_____

But if any of you lacks wisdom, let him ask
of God, who gives to all generously and
without reproach, and it will be given to
him.
James 1:5 (Read all of James 1)
New American Standard Bible

DEAR GOD,

And He said to him, "YOU SHALL LOVE THE LORD
YOUR GOD WITH ALL YOUR HEART, AND WITH ALL
YOUR SOUL, AND WITH ALL YOUR MIND."
Matthew 22:37 (Read all of Matthew 22)
New American Standard Bible

DEAR GOD,

_____
_____
_____
_____
_____
_____
_____
_____
_____
_____
_____
_____
_____
_____
_____
_____
_____
_____
_____

I have inherited Your testimonies forever,
For they are the joy of my heart.
Psalm 119:111 (Read all of Psalm 119)
New American Standard Bible

DEAR GOD,

Do
you not know that those who run in a race all
run, but [only] one receives the prize? Run
in such a way that you may win. so that,
after I have preached to others, I myself
will not be disqualified.
1 Corinthians 9:24-27 (Read all of
1 Corinthians 9)
New American Standard Bible

DEAR GOD,

_____
_____
_____
_____
_____
_____
_____
_____
_____
_____
_____
_____
_____

Instruct those who are rich
in this present world not to be conceited or
to fix their hope on the uncertainty of
riches, but on God, who richly supplies us
with all things to enjoy.
1 Timothy 6:17 (Read all of 1 Timothy 6)
New American Standard Bible

DEAR GOD,

_____
_____
_____
_____
_____
_____
_____
_____
_____
_____
_____
_____
_____
_____
_____
_____
_____
_____
_____
_____
_____
_____
_____

The young lions do lack and suffer hunger;
But they who seek the LORD shall not be in
want of any good thing.
Psalm 34:10 (Read all of Psalm 34)
New American Standard Bible

DEAR GOD,

_____
_____
_____
_____
_____
_____
_____
_____
_____
_____
_____
_____
_____

And this commandment we have from Him, that
the one who loves God should love his brother
also.
1 John 4:21 (Read all of 1 John 4)
New American Standard Bible

DEAR GOD,

_____
_____
_____
_____
_____
_____
_____
_____
_____
_____
_____
_____
_____
_____
_____
_____

And He summoned the crowd
with His disciples, and said to them, "If
anyone wishes to come after Me, he must deny
himself, and take up his cross and follow Me.
Mark 8:34 (Read all of Mark 8)
New American Standard Bible

DEAR GOD,

_____

_____

_____

_____

_____

_____

_____

_____

_____

_____

_____

_____

_____

_____

_____

_____

Your word is a lamp to my feet And a light to
my path.
Psalm 119:105 (Read all of Psalm 119)
New American Standard Bible

DEAR GOD,

A fool's lips bring strife, And his mouth
calls for blows.
Proverbs 18:6 (Read all of Proverbs 18)
New American Standard Bible

DEAR GOD,

_____

_____

_____

_____

_____

_____

_____

_____

_____

_____

_____

_____

_____

[Make sure that] your character is free from the love of money, being content with what you have; for He Himself has said, "I WILL NEVER DESERT YOU, NOR WILL I EVER FORSAKE YOU."
Hebrews 13:5 (Read all of Hebrews 13)
New American Standard Bible

DEAR GOD,

_____
_____
_____
_____
_____
_____
_____
_____
_____
_____
_____
_____
_____
_____
_____
_____

But
because of your stubbornness and unrepentant
heart you are storing up wrath for yourself
in the day of wrath and revelation of the
righteous judgment of God,
Romans 2:5 (Read all of Romans 2)
New American Standard Bible

DEAR GOD,

"Ask, and it will be given to you; seek, and
you will find; knock, and it will be opened
to you."
Matthew 7:7 (Read all of Matthew 7)
New American Standard Bible

DEAR GOD,

_____
_____
_____
_____
_____
_____
_____
_____
_____
_____
_____
_____
_____
_____
_____
_____
_____

" So
in the present case, I say to you, stay away
from these men and let them alone, for if
this plan or action is of men, it will be
overthrown;
Acts 5:38 (Read all of Acts 5)
New American Standard Bible

DEAR GOD,

The LORD is near to all who call upon Him, To
all who call upon Him in truth.
Psalm 145:18 (Read all of Psalm 145)
New American Standard Bible

DEAR GOD,

_____

For God has not given us a spirit of
timidity, but of power and love and
discipline.
2 Timothy 1:7 (Read all of 2 Timothy 1)
New American Standard Bible

DEAR GOD,

_____
_____
_____
_____
_____
_____
_____
_____
_____
_____
_____
_____
_____

"A new commandment I give to you, that you love
one another, even as I have loved you, that
you also love one another.
John 13:34 (Read all of John 13)
New American Standard Bible

DEAR GOD,

_____
_____
_____
_____
_____
_____
_____
_____
_____
_____
_____
_____
_____
_____
_____
_____
_____
_____
_____
_____
_____
_____

Pursue peace with all men, and the
sanctification without which no one will see
the Lord.
Hebrews 12:14 (Read all of Hebrews 12)
New American Standard Bible

DEAR GOD,

_____

_____

_____

_____

_____

_____

_____

_____

_____

_____

_____

_____

_____

As for every man to whom God has given riches
and wealth, He has also empowered him to eat
from them and to receive his reward andrejoice
in his labor; this is the gift of God.
Ecclesiastes 5:19 (Read all of
Ecclesiastes 5)
New American Standard Bible

DEAR GOD,

From everyone who has been given much, much
will be required; and to whom they entrusted
much, of him they will ask all the more.
Luke 12:48 (Read all of Luke 12)
New American Standard Bible

DEAR GOD,

_____
_____
_____
_____
_____
_____
_____
_____
_____
_____
_____
_____
_____
_____
_____
_____
_____

Let all that you do be done in love.
1 Corinthians 16:14 (Read all of
1 Corinthians 16)
New American Standard Bible

DEAR GOD,

_____
_____
_____
_____
_____
_____
_____
_____
_____
_____
_____
_____
_____
_____
_____
_____
_____
_____
_____

O God, You are my God; I shall seek You
earnestly; My soul thirsts for You, my flesh
yearns for You, In a dry and weary land where
there is no water.
Psalm 63:1 (Read all of Psalm 63)
New American Standard Bible

DEAR GOD,

_____
_____
_____
_____
_____
_____
_____
_____
_____
_____
_____
_____

"You
are the salt of the earth; but if the salt
has become tasteless, how can it be made
salty [again?] It is no longer good for
anything, except to be thrown out and
trampled under foot by men.
Matthew 5:13 (Read all of Matthew 5)
New American Standard Bible

DEAR GOD,

_____
_____
_____
_____
_____
_____
_____
_____
_____
_____
_____
_____
_____
_____
_____
_____

Now I
exhort you, brethren, by the name of our Lord
Jesus Christ, that you all agree and that
there be no divisions among you, but that you
be made complete in the same mind and in the
same judgment.
1 Corinthians 1:10 (Read all of
1 Corinthians 1)
New American Standard Bible

DEAR GOD,

_____
_____
_____
_____
_____
_____
_____
_____
_____
_____
_____
_____
_____
_____
_____
_____
_____
_____

To do righteousness and justice Is desired by
the LORD more than sacrifice.
Proverbs 21:3 (Read all of Proverbs 21)
New American Standard Bible

DEAR GOD,

_____
_____
_____
_____
_____
_____
_____
_____
_____
_____
_____
_____
_____
_____
_____
_____
_____
_____
_____

Do you not know? Have you not heard? The Everlasting God, the LORD, the Creator of the ends of the earth Does not become weary or tired. His understanding is inscrutable. Isaiah 40:28 (Read all of Isaiah 40) New American Standard Bible

DEAR GOD,

_____
_____
_____
_____
_____
_____
_____
_____
_____
_____
_____
_____
_____
_____
_____

So then, while we have opportunity, let us do good to all people, and especially to those who are of the household of the faith.
Galatians 6:10 (Read all of Galatians 6)
New American Standard Bible

DEAR GOD,

_____
_____
_____
_____
_____
_____
_____
_____
_____
_____
_____
_____
_____
_____
_____
_____
_____
_____
_____
_____
_____

At night my soul longs for You, Indeed, my
spirit within me seeks You diligently; For
when the earth experiences Your judgments The
inhabitants of the world learn righteousness.
Isaiah 26:9 (Read all of Isaiah 26)
New American Standard Bible

DEAR GOD,

_____
_____
_____
_____
_____
_____
_____
_____
_____
_____
_____
_____
_____
_____
_____
_____

A rebuke goes deeper into one who has
understanding Than a hundred blows into a
fool.
Proverbs 17:10 (Read all of Proverbs 17)
New American Standard Bible

DEAR GOD,

_____
_____
_____
_____
_____
_____
_____
_____
_____
_____
_____
_____
_____
_____
_____
_____
_____
_____
_____

What is the source of quarrels and conflicts
among you? Is not the source your pleasures
that wage war in your members?
James 4:1 (Read all of James 4)
New American Standard Bible

DEAR GOD,

_____
_____
_____
_____
_____
_____
_____
_____
_____
_____
_____
_____
_____

"If
there is a poor man with you, one of your
brothers, in any of your towns in your land
which the LORD your God is giving you, you
shall not harden your heart, nor close your
hand from your poor brother;
Deuteronomy 15:7 (Read all of Deuteronomy 15)
New American Standard Bible

DEAR GOD,

_____
_____
_____
_____
_____
_____
_____
_____
_____
_____
_____
_____
_____
_____
_____
_____
_____
_____

But flee from these things, you man of God,
and pursue righteousness, godliness, faith,
love, perseverance [and] gentleness.
1 Timothy 6:11 (Read all of 1 Timothy 6)
New American Standard Bible

DEAR GOD,

_____
_____
_____
_____
_____
_____
_____
_____
_____
_____
_____
_____
_____
_____
_____
_____
_____
_____

How can a young man keep his way pure? By
keeping [it] according to Your word.
Psalm 119:9 (Read all of Psalm 119)
New American Standard Bible

DEAR GOD,

_____
_____
_____
_____
_____
_____
_____
_____
_____
_____
_____
_____
_____
_____
_____
_____
_____
_____
_____

"Therefore everyone who hears these words of
Mine and acts on them, may be compared to a
wise man who built his house on the rock.
Matthew 7:24 (Read all of Matthew 7)
New American Standard Bible

DEAR GOD,

_____
_____
_____
_____
_____
_____
_____
_____
_____
_____
_____
_____
_____
_____
_____

"Do not fear, for I am with you; Do not
anxiously look about you, for I am your God.
I will strengthen you, surely I will help
you, Surely I will uphold you with My
righteous right hand."
Isaiah 41:10 (Read all of Isaiah 41)
New American Standard Bible

DEAR GOD,

_____
_____
_____
_____
_____
_____
_____
_____
_____
_____
_____
_____
_____
_____
_____
_____
_____
_____
_____
_____
_____

"But I say to you who hear, love your
enemies, do good to those who hate you,
Luke 6:27-28 (Read all of Luke 6)
New American Standard Bible

DEAR GOD,

_____
_____
_____
_____
_____
_____
_____
_____
_____
_____
_____
_____
_____
_____
_____
_____
_____
_____
_____

Pride [goes] before destruction, And a
haughty spirit before stumbling.
Proverbs 16:18 (Read all of Proverbs 16)
New American Standard Bible

DEAR GOD,

_____
_____
_____
_____
_____
_____
_____
_____
_____
_____
_____
_____
_____
_____
_____

Though the fig tree should not blossom And
There be no fruit on the vines, [Though] the
Yield of the olive should fail And the fields
produce no food, Though the flock should be
cut off from the fold And there be no cattle
in the stalls,
Habakkuk 3:17 (Read all of Habakkuk 3)
New American Standard Bible

DEAR GOD,

But at the end of that
period, I, Nebuchadnezzar, raised my eyes
toward heaven and my reason returned to me,
and I blessed the Most High and praised and
honored Him who lives forever; For His
dominion is an everlasting dominion, And His
kingdom [endures] from generation to
generation.
Daniel 4:34(Read all of Daniel 4)
New American Standard Bible

DEAR GOD,

"I amthe LORD, and there is no other; Besides
Me there is no God. I will gird you, though
You have not known Me;
Isaiah 45:5 (Read all of Isaiah 45)
New American Standard Bible

DEAR GOD,

_____
_____
_____
_____
_____
_____
_____
_____
_____
_____
_____
_____
_____
_____

But we all, with unveiled face, beholding as in a mirror the glory of the Lord, are being transformed into the same image from glory to glory, just as from the Lord, the Spirit.
2 Corinthians 3:18 (Read all of
2 Corinthians 3)
New American Standard Bible

DEAR GOD,

_____
_____
_____
_____
_____
_____
_____
_____
_____
_____
_____
_____
_____
_____
_____
_____
_____
_____
_____

"The thief comes only to steal and kill and
destroy; I came that they may have life, and
have [it] abundantly."
John 10:10 (Read all of John 10)
New American Standard Bible

DEAR GOD,

_____
_____
_____
_____
_____
_____
_____
_____
_____
_____
_____
_____
_____
_____

Be anxious for nothing, but in everything by
prayer and supplication with thanksgiving let
your requests be made known to God.
Philippians 4:6 (Read all of Philippians 4)
New American Standard Bible

DEAR GOD,

_____
_____
_____
_____
_____
_____
_____
_____
_____
_____
_____
_____
_____
_____
_____
_____
_____
_____
_____
_____
_____
_____

Not lagging behind in diligence, fervent in
spirit, serving the Lord.
Romans 12:11 (Read all of Romans 12)
New American Standard Bible

DEAR GOD,

"The steadfast of mind You will keep in
perfect peace, Because he trusts in You."
Isaiah 26:3 (Read all of Isaiah 26)
New American Standard Bible

DEAR GOD,

Therefore everyone who hears
these words of Mine and acts on them, may be
compared to a wise man who built his house on
the rock.
Matthew 7:24 (Read all of Matthew 7)
New American Standard Bible

DEAR GOD,

_____
_____
_____
_____
_____
_____
_____
_____
_____
_____
_____
_____
_____

"Know
therefore that the LORD your God, He is God,
the faithful God, who keeps His covenant and
His lovingkindness to a thousandth generation
with those who love Him and keep His
commandments."
Deuteronomy 7:9 (Read all of Deuteronomy 7)
New American Standard Bible

DEAR GOD,

_____
_____
_____
_____
_____
_____
_____
_____
_____
_____
_____
_____
_____
_____
_____
_____
_____

"Until now you have asked for nothing in My
name; ask and you will receive, so that your
joy may be made full."
John 16:24 (Read all of John 16)
New American Standard Bible

DEAR GOD,

_____

_____

_____

_____

_____

_____

_____

_____

_____

_____

_____

_____

_____

_____

_____

_____

Therefore let him who thinks he stands take
heed that he does not fall.
1 Corinthians 10:12 (Read all of
1 Corinthians 10)
New American Standard Bible

DEAR GOD,

Oh give thanks to the LORD, call upon His
name; Make known His deeds among the peoples.
Psalm 105:1 (Read all of Psalm 105)
New American Standard Bible

DEAR GOD,

_____
_____
_____
_____
_____
_____
_____
_____
_____
_____
_____
_____
_____

If someone says, "I love God," and hates his
brother, he is a liar; for the one who does
not love his brother whom he has seen, cannot
love God whom he has not seen.
1 John 4:20 (Read all of 1 John 4)
New American Standard Bible

DEAR GOD,

_____
_____
_____
_____
_____
_____
_____
_____
_____
_____
_____
_____
_____
_____
_____
_____
_____

Looking at them, Jesus said, "With people it is impossible, but not with God; for all things are possible with God."
Mark 10:27 (Read all of Mark 10)
New American Standard Bible

DEAR GOD,

_____

_____

_____

_____

_____

_____

_____

_____

_____

_____

_____

_____

_____

_____

_____

_____

_My son, if you will receive my words And
treasure my commandments within you,
Proverbs 2: (Read all of Proverbs 2)
New American Standard Bible

DEAR GOD,

To sum up, all of you be harmonious,
sympathetic, brotherly, kindhearted, and
humble in spirit.
1 Peter 3:8 (Read all of 1 Peter 3)
New American Standard Bible

DEAR GOD,

_____
_____
_____
_____
_____
_____
_____
_____
_____
_____
_____
_____
_____

"Therefore I say to you, all things for which
you pray and ask, believe that you have
received them, and they will be [granted]
you."
Mark 11:24 (Read all of Mark 11)
New American Standard Bible

DEAR GOD,

Rejoice in the Lord always; again I will say,
rejoice!
Philippians 4:4 (Read all of Philippians 4)
New American Standard Bible

DEAR GOD,

_____
_____
_____
_____
_____
_____
_____
_____
_____
_____
_____
_____

As he had come naked from his mother's womb, so will he return as he came. He will take nothing from the fruit of his labor that he can carry in his hand.
Ecclesiastes 5:15 (Read all of Ecclesiastes 5)
New American Standard Bible

DEAR GOD,

_____
_____
_____
_____
_____
_____
_____
_____
_____
_____
_____
_____
_____
_____
_____
_____
_____
_____
_____

By this we know that we
abide in Him and He in us, because He has
given us of His Spirit.
1 John 4:13 (Read all of 1 John 4)
New American Standard Bible

DEAR GOD,

_____
_____
_____
_____
_____
_____
_____
_____
_____
_____
_____
_____
_____
_____
_____

Who is the liar but the one who denies that
Jesus is the Christ? This is the antichrist,
the one who denies the Father and the Son.
1 John 2:22 (Read all of 1 John 2)
New American Standard Bible

DEAR GOD,

_____

_____

_____

_____

_____

_____

_____

_____

_____

_____

_____

_____

_____

_____

_____

_____

_____

_____

_____

_____

But thanks be to God, who gives us the
victory through our Lord Jesus Christ.
1 Corinthians 15:57 (Read all of
1 Corinthians 15)
New American Standard Bible

DEAR GOD,

_____
_____
_____
_____
_____
_____
_____
_____
_____
_____
_____
_____

You
are the salt of the earth; but if the salt
has become tasteless, how can it be made
salty [again?] It is no longer good for
anything, except to be thrown out and
trampled under foot by men."
Matthew 5:13 (Read all of Matthew 5)
New American Standard Bible

DEAR GOD,

_____

_____

_____

_____

_____

_____

_____

_____

_____

_____

_____

_____

_____

_____

_____

_____

_____

_____

Seek the LORD and His strength; Seek His face
continually.
Psalm 105:4 (Read all of Psalm 105)
New American Standard Bible

DEAR GOD,

_____
_____
_____
_____
_____
_____
_____
_____
_____
_____
_____
_____
_____

In hope against hope he believed, so that he might become a father of many nations according to that which had been spoken, "SO SHALL YOUR DESCENDANTS BE."
Romans 4:18 (Read all of Romans 4)
New American Standard Bible

DEAR GOD,

_____
_____
_____
_____
_____
_____
_____
_____
_____
_____
_____
_____
_____
_____
_____
_____
_____
_____
_____
_____
_____

He who conceals hatred [has] lying lips, And
he who spreads slander is a fool.
Proverbs 10:18 (Read all of Proverbs 10)
New American Standard Bible

DEAR GOD,

_____
_____
_____
_____
_____
_____
_____
_____
_____
_____
_____
_____
_____
_____
_____
_____

If we confess our sins, He is faithful and
righteous to forgive us our sins and to
cleanse us from all unrighteousness.
1 John 1:9 (Read all of 1 John 1)
New American Standard Bible

DEAR GOD,

_____
_____
_____
_____
_____
_____
_____
_____
_____
_____
_____
_____
_____
_____
_____
_____

Beloved, let us love one another, for love is from God; and everyone who loves is born of God and knows God.
1 John 4:7 (Read all of 1 John 4)
New American Standard Bible

DEAR GOD,

By this the love of God was manifested in us, that God has sent His only begotten Son into the world so that we might live through Him.
1 John 4:9 (Read all of 1 John 4)
New American Standard Bible

DEAR GOD,

"Let justice roll down like waters And
righteousness like an ever-flowing stream."
Amos 5:24 (Read all of Amos 5)
New American Standard Bible

DEAR GOD,

_____

_____

_____

_____

_____

_____

_____

_____

_____

_____

_____

For we do not want you to
be unaware, brethren, of our affliction which
came [to us] in Asia, that we were burdened
excessively, beyond our strength, so that we
despaired even of life;
2 Corinthians 1:8 (Read all of
2 Corinthians 1)
New American Standard Bible

DEAR GOD,

_____
_____
_____
_____
_____
_____
_____
_____
_____
_____
_____
_____
_____
_____
_____
_____
_____
_____
_____

My soul [waits] in silence for God only; From
Him is my salvation.
Psalm 62:1 (Read all of Psalm 62)
New American Standard Bible

DEAR GOD,

_____
_____
_____
_____
_____
_____
_____
_____
_____
_____
_____
_____
_____

"For God so loved the world, that He gave His
only begotten Son, that whoever believes in
Him shall not perish, but have eternal life."
John 3:16 (Read all of John 3)
New American Standard Bible

DEAR GOD,

_____
_____
_____
_____
_____
_____
_____
_____
_____
_____
_____
_____
_____
_____
_____
_____

For the one who sows to his own flesh will
from the flesh reap corruption, but the one
who sows to the Spirit will from the Spirit
reap eternal life.
Galatians 6:8 (Read all of Galatians 6)
New American Standard Bible

DEAR GOD,

_____
_____
_____
_____
_____
_____
_____
_____
_____
_____
_____
_____
_____
_____
_____

"This is My commandment, that you love one
another, just as I have loved you."
John 15:12 (Read all of John 15)
New American Standard Bible

DEAR GOD,

_____
_____
_____
_____
_____
_____
_____
_____
_____
_____
_____
_____
_____
_____
_____
_____
_____
_____

"For what will it profit a man if he gains the whole world and forfeits his soul? Or what will a man give in exchange for his soul?"
Matthew 16:26 (Read all of Matthew 16)
New American Standard Bible

DEAR GOD,

_____

_____

_____

_____

_____

_____

_____

_____

_____

_____

_____

_____

_____

_____

Walk in love, just as Christ also loved you
and gave Himself up for us, an offering and a
sacrifice to God as a fragrant aroma.
Ephesians 5:2 (Read all of Ephesians 5)
New American Standard Bible

DEAR GOD,

_____
_____
_____
_____
_____
_____
_____
_____
_____
_____
_____
_____
_____
_____
_____
_____

                    I say
to you, My friends, do not be afraid of those
who kill the body and after that have no more
              that they can do.
       Luke 12:4 (Read all of Luke 12)
         New American Standard Bible

DEAR GOD,

_____

_____

_____

_____

_____

_____

_____

_____

_____

_____

_____

_____

_____

Now
as they observed the confidence of Peter and
John and understood that they were uneducated
and untrained men, they were amazed, and
[began] to recognize them as having been with
Jesus.
Acts 4:13 (Read all of Acts 4)
New American Standard Bible

DEAR GOD,

_____
_____
_____
_____
_____
_____
_____
_____
_____
_____
_____
_____
_____
_____
_____
_____

You, therefore, who
teach another, do you not teach yourself? You
who preach that one shall not steal, do you
steal?
Romans 2:21 (Read all of Romans 2)
New American Standard Bible

DEAR GOD,

_____

_____

_____

_____

_____

_____

_____

_____

_____

_____

_____

_____

_____

_____

_____

_____

"He who has My commandments and keeps them is
the one who loves Me; and he who loves Me
will be loved by My Father, and I will love
him and will disclose Myself to him."
John 14:21 (Read all of John 14)
New American Standard Bible

DEAR GOD,

_____
_____
_____
_____
_____
_____
_____
_____
_____
_____
_____
_____
_____
_____
_____

[Make sure that] your character is free from the love of money, being content with what you have; for He Himself has said, "I WILL NEVER DESERT YOU, NOR WILL I EVER FORSAKE YOU,"
Hebrews 13:5 (Read all of Hebrews 13)
New American Standard Bible

DEAR GOD,

_____
_____
_____
_____
_____
_____
_____
_____
_____
_____
_____
_____
_____
_____

For the overseer must be above reproach as
God's steward, not self-willed, not quicktempere
not addicted to wine, not
pugnacious, not fond of sordid gain,
Titus 1:7 (Read all of Titus 1)
New American Standard Bible

DEAR GOD,

_____
_____
_____
_____
_____
_____
_____
_____
_____
_____
_____
_____
_____
_____
_____

So, as those who have been chosen of God,
holy and beloved, put on a heart of
compassion, kindness, humility, gentleness
and patience.
Colossians 3:12 (Read all of Colossians 3)
New American Standard Bible

DEAR GOD,

_____
_____
_____
_____
_____
_____
_____
_____
_____
_____
_____
_____
_____
_____
_____

Little children, let us not love with word or
with tongue, but in deed and truth.
1 John 3:18 (Read all of 1 John 3)
New American Standard Bible

DEAR GOD,

_____
_____
_____
_____
_____
_____
_____
_____
_____
_____
_____
_____
_____
_____
_____
_____
_____

"Greater love has no one than this, that one
lay down his life for his friends."
John 15:13 (Read all of John 15)
New American Standard Bible

DEAR GOD,

_____

_____

_____

_____

_____

_____

_____

_____

_____

_____

_____

_____

_____

_____

_____

That I may know Him and the power of His
resurrection and the fellowship of His
sufferings, being conformed to His death.
Philippians 3:10 (Read all of Philippians 3)
New American Standard Bible

DEAR GOD,

_____
_____
_____
_____
_____
_____
_____
_____
_____
_____
_____
_____
_____
_____
_____
_____
_____

Jesus said to her, "I am the resurrection and
the life; he who believes in Me will live
even if he dies,
John 11:25 (Read all of John 11)
New American Standard Bible

DEAR GOD,

_____
_____
_____
_____
_____
_____
_____
_____
_____
_____
_____
_____
_____
_____
_____
_____
_____

With all humility and gentleness, with
patience, showing tolerance for one another
in love,
Ephesians 4:2 (Read all of Ephesians 4)
New American Standard Bible

DEAR GOD,

_____
_____
_____
_____
_____
_____
_____
_____
_____
_____
_____
_____
_____
_____
_____
_____
_____

Commit your way to the LORD, Trust also in
Him, and He will do it.
Psalm 37:5-6 (Read all of Psalm 37)
New American Standard Bible

www.ingramcontent.com/pod-product-compliance
Lightning Source LLC
Chambersburg PA
CBHW021218090426
42740CB00006B/271